Before YOU "Litigate YOUR Rights"

During Police Encounter - Ask yourself three 3 questions

Jon Moses

"Treat the Truth like Chips, Let Them Fall where They May."
Author ~ JM

ISBN: 9798902715313

DEDICATION

Dedicated to various law enforcement officers both men and women across the globe who have chosen to serve and protect their fellow citizens and, in that process, lost their very precious lives. Thank you to those very brave and honorable men and women, who serve with courage and commitment to excellence, and did not cut corners in service, did not usurp their authority, and did not compromise their fellow citizens who were often at disadvantages in their clear understanding of the applicable traffic laws.

To the families that these brave officers left behind, thank you for your own private service that are burden of a lifetime. May you find peace in knowing that your loved ones did not die in vain but in the utmost Biblical calling that a man would lay down his life in service to other human beings.

And to those who lost their lives due to bad policing, may you rest in God's perfect peace. We, the people, failed you somehow through lack of proper guidance at earlier stages of life. Moving forward, perhaps Driver's Education classes should focus more on traffic stop rules, as well as prioritizing obedience to the law and respect for officers as aggressively as the focus on learning how to steer vehicles.

May reading a copy of this book be a soothing console to all families left behind due to mere traffic encounters.

CONTENTS

ACKNOWLEDGMENTS

Why do majority of drivers promptly slow down on city or major highways when a police car is sported riding slightly ahead in traffic? Because drivers knew that the person behind the wheel is duly commissioned to enforce traffic laws. The officer might be off-duty at the time, however; he can still pull you over and for that, many are not tempted to speed ahead of his vehicle. The moment the officer exited; everyone picks up speed as if collectively saying, "**There goes the man.**"

And do you ever wonder why it happens that way? **It is because the presence of the police car represents authority**. Sometimes though, there might be a driver tempted to dry faster than the officer who is purposefully driving as a pace car for everyone else. Then suddenly, off goes the blue lights and sirens. We all have egos deep as the depth of Niagara Falls. Regardless of each individual's professional occupation, there is a hidden ego in all of us. Just that many have self-control, while some others do not. Some officers might ignore such a move, while for others; it just might mean that it is the time to take out the summons.

By law, anything over speed limit, at the discretion of the officer, you can be ticketed. And when the siren or blue lights go off, your safe bet is to simply comply. **Arguing the legality of any stop on the roadside would be lacking common sense**. It's what Gen Z coined as FAFO on the web. Hello AI, what does the acronym FAFO means?[1] FAFO is an internet slang acronym for "F*** Around And Find Out," meaning if someone behaves carelessly or provocatively, they will face the negative consequences.

While someone may decide to fight a police officer by the roadside, the officer is only a tiny part of the system such a person will have to contend with at a later date. Remember that fighting the officers **authorize to enforce laws** of all types including traffic laws only give you a temporary pleasure. He is a tiny part of the system – Would you also fight **The judge** too? With unruly behavior in the courtroom, the judge at the stroke of a pen could cause you more pain than you can handle even without a weapon. **You have more than fifty percent chance of winning in the courts**, and **one hundred percent chance** that **you will lose** on your roadside's righteous litigation. So, comply!

---

[1] . Hello AI, what does the acronym FAFO means?[1]

During Police Encounter - Ask yourself these 3 questions

During Police Encounter - Ask yourself these 3 questions

CHAPTER 1. **DID WE FAIL THEM?**

Not so long ago, a schoolteacher would walk into the classroom and every child, including the most stubborn child in the class, would all behave and get into learning mold because there were incentives and disincentives for behaviors that comply with the teacher's instructions and those that will have it their way or no way at all.

What do these two professions - police officers and schoolteachers have in common? They both represents authority.

Teachers were more so in the life of a child during developmental years, and officers in the life of those children that either were never taught or refused to learn, have some type of disabilities that restrict the ability to learn like other children or just got caught up with the wrong crowd. And once these children transition into adults, the ones in the group home or other residential facilities are released into society to fend for themselves. Something they have never done in life before the age of 18 or 21 in some states.

Some of these formerly youngsters, now bonafide adults, would end up in county jails within their communities after conviction of misdemeanor offenses which carries lighter sentences. Most could receive jail sentence ranging from six months and sometimes up to two years and be released back to the society with what is termed as "good behavior" after serving about three or four months of the total sentence. The hard-core offenders who commits crimes like

assault, assault with deadly weapon, burglary, distribution of drugs and drugs paraphernalia, kidnapping, robbery, theft, and theft by taking, possession of stolen property, rape, and you know it, eventually murder usually end up in state or federal prison for a lot longer as most of these offenses are categorized as felonies.

Next stop for most of these guys after serving their time is usually halfway houses as some have no previous or stable place to return to, while some others just chose not to return to the same community they left behind upon incarceration. Some, not all halfway houses hardly ever have knowledgeable staff on duty who genuinely care to make necessary changes to prevent guarantee return back into the system. In a sense, hopelessness becomes the norm. Once hopelessness sets in, the desire to commit other crimes becomes much more present than the need to do right.

Naturally, with this state of mind, one can see why obeying simple command could become a perplexing task. It is why this chapter asked the rhetorical question, "Did we fail them?" And of course, we did without a doubt! It is clear that not everyone that failed to follow simple instructions are mentally challenged, however; some are and it is hard to decipher who is who during a brief traffic encounter with law enforcements. So, it is best to try first to de-escalate as much as possible for a safer, better outcome.

During Police Encounter - Ask yourself these 3 questions

The late 1980's through early 1990's saw a spike in drug distribution and usage due to so many people thinking it is a way to close the gap between the rich and the poor by because a drug dealer. What was so unfortunate back then was that the drugs presented the very first opportunity for Black-on-Black crimes. The dealers were Black, the users were also Black, and the community that was wrecked were Black communities.

And there was no one screaming that Black lives matter then. So many beautiful people lost their lives, parents lost their child and some lost their children to the drug epidemic. As society, we failed them again. As young people were dying due to drug overdose, due to drug related killings, entire neighborhood was made desolate as people moved their families out to a peaceful area. Many homes were simply abandoned, and the homes stayed that way for years.

There was no community developments in most ground zero of drug epidemic and all the most famous community organizer in Chicago, IL, and others in Baltimore, MD, as well as in Buffalo, NY did not show up to lend a helping hand.

Coincidentally, a lot of products were imported from China that were not affordable to young people, but they do see other children who came from affluent family wearing those things. And without proper training to understand that you work for what you want and not kill for it, many children were killed for their name brand sneakers and name

During Police Encounter - Ask yourself these 3 questions

brand fashion wears. Wasting a life so you can have what the person you murdered on your body came from the deepest of ignorance. But it happened.

Theft of Sneakers, boom box, electronics of all sorts were quite common, and many lost their lives over these casual possessions. Two famous people made two uniquely unwise interdictions into the drug crime wave. One, an unelected First Lady of the United State came from the heart, offering her absolute best solutions to the problem. But it was destined to fail from the get-go. The other, a sitting United States Senator and Chairman of the Senate Judiciary Committee also offered his best solution – he authored and sponsored a law that send many young people prisons for life.

First Lady Nancy Reagan gave a speech at the Roosevelt Room, in Washington, DC address the drug problems plaguing the nation. Here is what she said:

Mrs. Reagan's Remarks "Just Say No" Week Signing Ceremony Roosevelt Room Tuesday, May 20, 1986

At the beginning of this year, someone asked me if I wanted to make a New Year's wish and I said, "Yes." And it was that I'd like to see every young person in the world join the "Just Say No To Drugs" Club. Well, just the fact that Congress has proclaimed "Just Say No" week and in light of all the activities taking place, my wish is well on the way to

During Police Encounter - Ask yourself these 3 questions

corning true.

I am so proud of all the young people, the parents, the citizens in cities and towns across this nation, the government, and everyone else who is helping to create what I believe is the final solution to this problem. And that is a way to teach every one of our children to "just say no" to drugs. The future of the world lies in their hands, and we all must come together~ in their name to end drug and alcohol abuse once and for all. Again, thank you so much for what you are doing and for joining us today. [2]

Again, the Late First Lady had a great intentions and we can just leave it at that. A few years later, Senator Joe Biden, as Chairman of the Senate Judiciary Committee played a key role in drafting "The 1994 Violent Crime Control and Law Enforcement Act", which included a federal "three strikes" law that mandated a life sentence for a third serious or violent felony conviction. This law is a controversial part of his legacy and a major point of discussion regarding mass incarceration in America". [3]

Instead of providing solution to solving the crime issues in its infancy, the Senator, during another Senate hearing in 1977, expresses that

---

[2] https://www.reaganlibrary.gov/public/digitallibrary/smof/speechwriting-speechdrafts/box-437/40-534-5711755-437-001-2018.pdf
[3] https://www.cnn.com/videos/politics/2019/06/06/joe-biden-defends-1994-crime-bill-zeleny-pkg-lead-vpx.cnn

During Police Encounter - Ask yourself these 3 questions

"Unless we do something about this, my children are going to grow up in a jungle, the jungle being a racial jungle with tensions having built so high that it is going to explode at some point". And it is this mindset, not concern for care or justice; but for self-aggrandizement and family preservation that Senator Joe Biden sponsored the legislation that went scotch earth on young Black children in the inner cities of New York, Chicago, Philadelphia, Detroit, and Los Angeles among others in 1994.

Fast forward thirty years later, the same politician from the nineties who wanted the harshest punishment for any crime major or minor, misdemeanors or felonies; now wanted no punishment at all to atone for past err in judgment. And law makers can change their minds based on where and how the wind is blowing, the tragic thing is that the clients always remain the same.

At the turn of the century right following the passing of the 1994 major crime bill authored by Senator Joe Biden during the Clinton presidency; restrictions started popping up left and right on how much discipline is just and many small-time streets level drug dealers and users ended up in prison for third offenses no matter what it was. That is because the name of the laws was "three strikes you are out" permanently. Definitely inhumane but that was the sentiment back then as people are tired of crimes and criminals disturbing their personal peace.

But there was a better way, just that it was never evaluated prior to the law. So, the law ended up creating more criminals than rescue from

During Police Encounter - Ask yourself these 3 questions

their pain and sufferings in the inner city.

It is hard for most programs that provide services to children and some emotionally challenged individuals to attract and maintain quality staff that can truly impact the children and young adults they care for. Why? Because the pay is poor and the schedules are tedious. So, most people just obtain the job to pad their resumes as a stepping stone to something better. I should know because for over twenty-five years I had progressed from program counselor to manager, ultimately; to program director with shifts that prevents time off for most major holidays and weekends. Those who have the love of the clients would stay and many would simply move on creating lack of stability in the lives of the troubled clients that you might encounter one day.

To prevent some of the incidents we are facing in our community with regards to challenges to authority, those kinds of programs needs qualified staff to manage and provide care as well as paygrade that is as good as what a man working as a mechanic or delivery guy would make. Afterall, what is more important in the scheme of things.

The client just goes out with the motion. Hence, prison recidivism skyrocketed. Men and women who genuinely cares and wanted to help could not get support, financial or otherwise; however, those with connections usually gets funding for programs of which they have no mental connections on how to make needed changes, but obtaining funding was just as simple as ABC. So, the problems of the young men

During Police Encounter - Ask yourself these 3 questions

in the inner city just go into a vicious circle. Go in, come out, repeat the process. This is another way that society failed the youths of thirty years ago. This is the way it was. Today, it is quite different except it has not gotten better.

True leaders looks for problems to solve; bad leaders create problems and leave them behind for others solve while they go about boasting about what an excellent job they did. With an astute leader in place in the 1990's, America would not have lost the war on drugs and just say no and three strikes you're out would not have happened. According to CDC (Center for Disease Control), as gathered by Google AI; between 1988, 1989, and 1990, 15,000 deaths were attributed to drug overdose and drug poisoning. [4]

Deaths Due to Drug Transactions (Homicides)

It is difficult to ascertain the exact number of deaths specifically tied to "drug transactions" as official statistics categorize deaths as homicides, but research clearly links the rise in the homicide rate during this period to the emergence and expansion of crack cocaine markets.

- The crack epidemic dramatically increased the number of Americans using cocaine in the mid-1980s and led to substantial increases in violence.

[4] Deaths due to drug poisoning and drug overdose between 1988 and 1990

During Police Encounter - Ask yourself these 3 questions

- Researchers estimate that the **murder rate for young Black males doubled** shortly after crack's introduction into a city (roughly 1984-1994). The overall homicide rate for this demographic nearly doubled during this period, while it remained flat for older Black men.

- The overall U.S. homicide rate peaked in 1991 at 10.1 per 100,000 population. The specific number of homicides nationally in 1991 was likely around 24,700 (based on a population of ~244 million).

- Much of the increase in violent crime in the 1980s and early 1990s was attributed to a doubling of the rate of homicides by juveniles, which was linked to the crack trade.

Dealing with drug makers and drug kingpin is a not task for the weak at heart. The damage they do on a daily basis is unforgiveable. Just ask those that the epidemic have affected how they feel about taking no actions and appease or taking strong actions to destroy those responsible for the loss of their loved ones. Strong actions that destroy these makers and distributors of killer drugs would make sure that we do not go back the eighty's and ninety's again. Doing that means we will not fail our young people again.

During Police Encounter - Ask yourself these 3 questions

CHAPTER 2 – TEACHERS & POLICE OFFICERS

For not too long ago, teachers and law enforcement officers represent valuable authority in knowledge and security. But wait! What is the actual definition of authority and why is it such that the mere mention of it aggravates people these days. According to Merriam-Webster's dictionary, authority is defined as "Power to influence or command thought, opinion, or behaviors." [5]

Based on this simple definition, the notion of authority is not such a terrible thing after all.

Wherever the children call home before coming to school and into the classrooms; it is safe to conclude that each child has a parent, caretakers or designated custodians such as social services, residential facilities, group homes among others who are solely responsible for the children's care on a daily basis. That means these parents or care takers are the ultimate authority over the children's lives unless a crime is committed which could rapidly transfer that authority to governmental hands starting from social welfare services all the way to Department of Corrections depending upon the age of the person.

And for years, these collective parents-care takers had the ability to discipline the child within their care without any objections. In so far,

[5] Merriam-Webster's dictionary

During Police Encounter - Ask yourself these 3 questions

the disciplinary measures taken did not translate into abuse or unethical punishment. The result of such power, yes, power over the child's mental growth was very obvious. It is almost like a quid-pro-quo.

However, when the children are in school, the school administration from Librarians to teachers all the way to the Principals all have the power to influence by first educating the child, and if that fails, then it gets elevated into disciplinary actions as appropriate. And this power is express and has no ambiguity unless discipline crosses over into abuse.

It has always been this way. And it has worked so well that leaders were produced through both public and private school systems where discipline was key in maintaining higher achievements in schools.

The group of people in the example below did extra ordinary things in life that many could only dream about. These were winners through and through. They did not permit society to fail them. Every mother would want their son or daughters to marry any of these people in their prime. They all took potentially negative situation and turned it into a thing of beauty. All you have to do is take a quick minute to look at their remarkable lives starting from Justice Marshall, the first African American man to sit on the nation's highest court in history to the real deal Fannie Lou, a sharecropper who dropped out only to make history in so many facets of life.

The power of education opened doors for many of them, while one

During Police Encounter - Ask yourself these 3 questions

had no formal education but was a sure-fire goal getter. Let us find out about these resilient six.

1.The late Supreme Court Justice Thurgood Marshall, a civil rights lawyer who became the first African American on the United States Supreme Court as an Associate Justice. It is so easy to overlook this man's accomplishments because it happened so no big deal. But the time it happened, for those who were around to witness it, the feeling they expressed was like witnessing Joe Louis, the Heavyweight Champion of the World beat the German Max Schmeling in 1938 for the world title in Chicago. It was a sense of the biggest national pride as the west prepare for war against the Nazi. The fight that united Americans behind Joe Louis, aka the Bronx Bomber irrespective of the racial conflicts.

2. Marine Corp Aviator and later Senator from the State of Ohio who went to the Moon, Senator John Herschel Glenn. From becoming one of the first man ever to go to space as an Aviator for the United States NASA (National Aeronautics and Space Administration) to later becoming a United States Senator from the great State of Ohio, and he concluded that life's journey as a Presidential Candidate. What a fulfilled life.

3. The Rev. Dr. Martin Luther King Jr. who, at an early age, because of the quality of his education, from Morehouse College in Atlanta, led the

nation's most powerful civil rights movement at a young age. This man was a visionary in the like of Moses from the Bible. His oratory skills and passion for justice sets him apart from all the rest. His messages were non-violent, God centered. One of those messages that the nation seems to have forgotten and is so relevant today as if he had just given it five minutes ago. Here is an excerpt from the I have a Dream speech, "I have a dream that my four little children will one day live in a nation where they will not be judged by the color of their skin but by their character." One can only wonder what Dr. King would say today!

4. President Donald John Trump, 45th and 47th President of the United States whose story of becoming president as a total political novice and outsider is remarkable but would only become obvious as time passes on when the history of America's presidency is written. In Africa, Asia, Middle East, Europe, Eastern European blocs; President's Trump's influence is just simply remarkable. History begins today and must be told with open mind and desire to embrace the truth.

5. Chief Obafemi Awolowo, a Nigerian Leader who introduced free primary school education for all in 1955, and was later sent to prison for ten years by the tribalistic and race-conscious Northern zealot government of Tafawa Balewa. He was later released by the Military government of General Yakubu Gowon and served as the Nigeria's Commissioner of Finance. This man was a very remarkable human being. Chief Awolowo was Nelson Mandela before Mandela's time.

During Police Encounter - Ask yourself these 3 questions

6. Fannie Lou Hamer, though less educated than all persons cited before her, she dropped out at age twelve while working as a sharecropper in Mississippi. She was credited as been smart naturally and later she educated herself through diligent study, and received several honorary degrees for her activism. There is a famous quote attributed to Fannie Lou and you might have heard it before. "I'm sick and tired of being sick and tired." This quote was from the speech she gave during the 1964 Democratic National Convention in Atlantic City, New Jersey. She was also the last born of twenty children in her family.

When we have allowed the public-school systems to work without injecting political ideology of any kind, the school system in the United States is second to none. And when our laws are allowed to be enforced without self-serving, hate mongering, anti-climactic disagreements, this nation has the best system anywhere in the world. Unless you are just thinking out loud for clicks, no one should be willing to give it up and go elsewhere. It will be missed within the first few days.

All the aforementioned extremely successful individuals above were taught and influenced by one or more teachers over their school days. And it is likely one primary reason most children that have the opportunity to go to school, and who allowed the teachers to influence and educate them, have success rates in life in the high percentile. Of course, the measuring stick for this is nothing extremely scientific. It is measured by lower crime statistics and how well society functioned

During Police Encounter - Ask yourself these 3 questions

back then. More family stabilities, more financial stabilities, sound employment stabilities, and visible spiritual stabilities in society.

Education was emphasized above many things to do with one's time as a youth. Many families worked hard, some even struggled hard to ensure that their children would have the best education they can afford. In those days, an educated child can lift up a family of three from abject poverty because of education and hard work.

Yes, there was no internet back in the sixties, seventies and even in the eighties. The gaming systems back then were Atari, Tandy, Pacman, and Foosball amongst others. More time were dedicated to being the best and not trying to look like a million bucks by wearing fake gold chains, wilding as was made famous during early nineties.

Another thing that totally changed over the last twenty-five years is that schools are no longer able to discipline a child for any discipline-worthy activities. Behaviors like talking in the classrooms, talking while the teacher is talking, initiating fights in the classroom and blatant disregard for the school's principals.

Later in life, these disruptive students ended up becoming the responsibilities of our law enforcement officers. It is a monumental task that has the potential to wreak havoc when it is not professionally managed. And in many instances, it has. Collectively, as a society; we failed those young people we referred to as children during the late

During Police Encounter - Ask yourself these 3 questions

nineties and early in the new millennium who are now in their thirties and twenties and have little or no foundation in how to communicate and lack basic conflict resolution skills.

Every misunderstanding is considered disrespect, what should be given of respect for an elderly person is quickly interpreted by the youngster as a disrespect to him or her. It is a total role reversal unlike anything that the world has ever seen before. As it was famously asked by Nino Brown, played by Wesley Snipes in the movie New Jack City, "Am I my brother's keepers?" [6]

And of course, the original question was asked in the Bible after Cain had killed his brother Abel. Late, God questioned Cain about the very first such occurrence of murder in the Bible.

Literarily, we set our youth to fail by removing basic discipline from classrooms. As adults, you know what it was like to be disciplined in schools back in the fifties through the seventies. Nope, it was not abuse by all means, it was teaching a young person how to become a man and the young gal how to become a woman with sense of directions and purposeful living. Not only did we refuse to allow authority figures in school to do what they were hired to do, we also hogtied the parents at

---

[6] In *New Jack City*, the line "Am I my brother's keeper?" is screamed by the drug lord Nino Brown (Wesley Snipes) during a heated argument, especially after he betrays and murders his own crew members, famously prompting his followers to yell back, "Yes I am!" to affirm their loyalty.

During Police Encounter - Ask yourself these 3 questions

home by encouraging the child to be rebellious if anyone says or does something he or she finds offensive.

Well, the discipline that was omitted for the seven, eight, nine-year-olds in school, has now come home to roast in the society by twenty and thirty-something-year olds running wild on our streets. We encouraged and guided them to live as independent adults while they were yet children just genuinely wanting supervision and guidance; we misled them to respond to things as only adults should do, and we coarse all adults to take the role of onlookers instead of bonafide guidance.

Those children that are now thirty years old have been acting their age since before puberty. And they are wreaking havoc on our streets, disrespecting our authorized authorities, failing to maintain basic standards and the only thing they know is what we exposed them to all along. Be a man! Stand up for yourself and prove your manhood!

Unfortunately, the society-sponsored dereliction of duty is still going on today and there seems to be no hope on the horizon. It has gotten worse that professional teachers are teaching children to lie about so many things to include their sexual orientation while also encouraging behaviors that were contrary twenty-five years ago as mainstream events. All of these contribute to the upside nation. So, we will continue to deal with the repercussions of our misguided role in the life of our precious children until we wake up to see the enormous damage we have caused.

During Police Encounter - Ask yourself these 3 questions

In the interim, let us recognize that even as a free country, anything we do outside of our homes deserves some form of enforcement as not all citizens would obey the law of safety and peaceful co-habitation with others. If America cannot nurture and control our future by controlling and discipline our youths, then we have no future. We are likely to go by the way of the ancient Romans, the British Empire, and many other has been nations.

It is to be noted that this failure within our society crosses the bounds of race, color, ideology, and spiritual dispensations. It is of the failure of true humanity as we individually chase happiness while our collective good lacks behind.

The roles of teachers and police officers have been totally diminished over the last couple of decades. First, the downward spiral of the teaching profession, by those who turn teachers and the teaching professionals into a political football to achieve a certain goals that is neither friendly nor future focus. With policies that allows children to be a mini teacher. Children have autonomy in the classrooms to do as please with impunity. With so much independence, why even send our young to school! This is definitely a wrong move.

With the law enforcement, it is the constant talk of racism for every attempt to enforce laws that are already on the books. Enforcement is criminalized while those who commits crime are giving a pass to continue their behaviors unhindered.

During Police Encounter - Ask yourself these 3 questions

Historically speaking, nations which lacked the types of authority that teachers and law enforcement agencies represent, and projects; run a chaotic social environment. Chaotic enough that most people who could afford to move usually do. A nation where teachers have no power or authority over basic daily guidelines in the classrooms and law enforcement officers who have no power or authority over the basic maintenance of society's law cannot stand together for long.

Furthermore, once these too professions lose their inherent authority as the arbiters of Knowledge and Law and Order in their respective fields; the first thing to surfer would be the elements of truth. Likewise, it trickles down to all other areas of life including the seven fundamental literacies vis-à-vis Home Basic Literacy, Early Literacy, Civic and Social Literacy, Digital Literacy, Financial Literacy, Health Literacy, and Legal Literacy.

During Police Encounter - Ask yourself these 3 questions

CHAPTER 3. **ASK YOURSELF**

As the blue lights and sirens blast away behind you and you are contemplating what to do and or say, quickly ask yourself these few questions. Doing so would block out the noise of agitators who only want to see you fail at the expense of their social media postings. Failure to do so would cause you to become famous for all the wrong reasons.

1. Am I deputize by the society to enforce local, state, or federal laws in this jurisdiction where I am being stopped? (Or in other words, am I driving the patrol car with a badge, a teaser, an handcuff, a gun and the right to haul someone off to jail)
2. Have I been sworn in to serve and protect this community, town, city, or state where I am been stopped? (Simplify – am I the sheriff or jailor in these community)

And lastly, right or wrong,

a. a. Would I rather get a citation to appear in court on a future date if the officer deem that as a necessary measure to secure my immediate release so I can continue my day? b. Would I prefer a free ride and wait to post bond plus all other unknown jail conditions for the next 24 hours or maybe more? (more, if the arrest was on Saturday, you might have to stay in jail until Monday to have a hearing before the judge).

During Police Encounter - Ask yourself these 3 questions

c. Or am I prepare to be transported to coroner's facility on the ice cold bench tonight to prove something to myself and others?

If answer to any of these questions is yes, kindly stop reading, put this book down, and follow your master plan. If the answer to any of the questions is no, but you have an issue with law enforcement officers duly authorised to enforced the law, to serve and to protect citizens like yourself on behalf of all of us, to detain and or arrest; then the probability that you need this book is greater than average. And then you definitely have to change your circle of influencers.Influencers you might label as green snakes under the green grass. This has no benefit except it is good at camoflauging.

You see my brother, my sister, we all have just one life to live. Let no one, no ideology, even a misguided theology cause you to lose yours. You can be right, but certainly; you do not want to be dead right.

Too many times, police encounter that should be resolved amicably between two people is quickly escalated because of built in animosity from previous wrongs involving none of the two people involved in the current events. And usually if the current events, which is the traffic stop; is viewed through the lens of a century old oppression from those that are no longer around to bear the punishment, nothing would ever get better, and many innocent people would end up losing their lives or end up in prison for one person's actions.

During Police Encounter - Ask yourself these 3 questions

We have leaders that only shows up when tragedy strikes. Only shows up to check if they can see their shadows like General Punxsutawney Phil, the highly famous groundhog from Punxsutawney, Pennsylvania to predict how long the winter would last. Soon as there is a police shooting regardless of the circumstances, you will have the airwaves dominated for days if not weeks.

Once that case is handled whichever way, the noise settles down, and the groundhog leaders disappeared! There is no new coalition established to help the young men who are the constant victims of the traffic tragedies prior to becoming victims. Help shows up when there is some kind of benefits to the leaders in form of financial rewards or pollical clout. In today's environment with traffic deaths by young Black youths, what would Dr. Martin Luther King Jr. do?

The real help that these young people needed to hear that might change their mindset in traffic stops is covered up with political rhetoric about race which does nothing but stares up anger towards law enforcement officers. And all these does is to perpetually continues the anger and frustration. The power of great leaders cannot be under-estimated so is the negative power of leaders that fail to apply their common-sense each and every time there is an incident of national interests.

Too many times, police encounters that should be resolved smoothly, and relatively quickly has many times resulted into an instant tragedy – in fact, a national tragedy. And encounter that did not only proved

During Police Encounter - Ask yourself these 3 questions

deadly for one, but the consequent actions by other citizens has ended the life of many more following riots and protests that usually followed. And most if not all the deaths post the initial incident happens at the hands of rioters decrying initial police killing. And the lives lost during the protests are just quietly, simply forgotten. This has to stop as many mothers have buried too many young lives too soon.

What is baffling is that IT HASN'T ALWAYS BEEN THIS WAY. And the changes is not citizen focused. Otherwise, there would not be an attempt by one group trying to monetize and politicize police-public relations tragedy. When it becomes citizen focus, there would be unity of purpose and unified voice. Otherwise, the problem would never be solved.

The mothers who have lost their children would be in the Amen corner because of the permanent pain that they have experienced with the loss of a child or adult child at times. So, to the God-fearing leaders, mothers, and every driver that would decide not to comply with police instructions, is it worth it? Ask yourself, is it worth it to turn what could have been an unremarkable ten-minute traffic stop into a tragedy that will require a hearse to transport a body to the morgue?. I should hope not.

During Police Encounter - Ask yourself these 3 questions

CHAPTER 4 **COMMANDS & COMMON SENSE**

Commands are just that - commands. Commands are not intended as an option. Just like the stop signs on our roads and highways command us to stop, stop means stop literally. As command to stop is based on the reality that when one failed to stop, it could mean a tragedy for others who are simply obeying the command to stop or go.

Command does not depend on the mood we are in, how we feel, and if the instructor giving the directives is short, tall, or lightweight physically compared to how gigantic we look. And in fact, it does not depend on whether the law enforcement officer giving the command is Black, White, Asian, Indian, or African which in fact will be subjective.

Commands should not be confused with questions which require a yes, no or maybe answer. The officer would say, "would you like to give me your driver's please?" Rather, it will be, "your driver's license! Once you have this process in your mind before the officer(s) approached your vehicle, the rest should be simple enough to get you moving on your goals for that day. The only decision you need to make is to comply.

Obeying commands, any commands, either from law enforcement officers on the side of the road, or from a bailiff in the courtroom, or flight attendants on an airplane high in the sky; or even from our doctor's prescribed medicine with specific dosage instructions, not only simplifies our lives but absolutely saves it. Period.

During Police Encounter - Ask yourself these 3 questions

Consider this, your doctor prescribed medicine for you to help you overcome some illness. The pharmacy filled the medication with specific instructions; in this case we would use specific commands. On the label , it says take three tablets three times a day for xyz illness. If you decide to take three tablets once in the morning as opposed to one tablet three times daily, you may need an ambulance to save your life.

Commands are instructions that need to be taken seriously by simply obeying. And the tool that is requires to understand any command is just our most valuable asset – common sense. Preparing for this project, I consulted the web to get a universal definition of common sense. Though I am aware of its true definition, having a source for others to verify is important. I decided to look into what role the application of common sense, or lack of it plays in most traffic stops and its outcomes. So, I asked, "AI, why is common sense vital in our day-to-day activities? [7]

"Common sense is vital because it enables us to make sound, practical decisions, navigate social situations, and avoid unnecessary risks. It provides a framework for problem-solving, evaluating potential consequences, and making logical conclusions based on practical experience and an understanding of the world. This ability to apply practical judgment is a key aspect of daily functioning and a valuable

---

[7] Command - AI, why is common sense vital in our day-to-day activities?

During Police Encounter - Ask yourself these 3 questions

"soft skill" in both personal and professional life.

Why common sense is vital.

- Practical decision-making:

It helps you evaluate situations and consequences to make good choices, rather than impulsive or foolish ones. This can be as simple as knowing not to order the largest fries when trying to eat healthy, or understanding not to put a pizza back in the oven on its cardboard base."

Now that AI has simplified some of the reasons why common sense is vital, lets proceed and evaluate how applying common sense can help save lives in a casual encounter with law enforcement officers who are fully sanctioned by society to enforce the smallest infractions categorized as misdemeanors to the highest ranging offences such as felonies with various classes.

Commands you are likely to hear from most officers conducting a traffic stop for any and all interactions are not suggestive commands but commands to obey. And obeying these simple commands, would get you on your way either home, your planned appointments, and or being place in temporary custody by the officer or officers of the law at the location until a fast resolution of the circumstances can be determine and resolve either by a Judge at a later date and time.

During Police Encounter - Ask yourself these 3 questions

Forcefully exercising your constitutional rights on the roadside means that you have chosen to wrestle control of the traffic stop away from the designated officer of the law. Mind you, in the history of traffic stops; taking ownership of a traffic stop initiated by officer of the law has never favored anyone but the officer(s) who conducted the traffic stop. Disagreement with how or what the officer did in conducting the stop would not be resolved between you and the officer on the roadside.

If you decided to protest perceived wrongful stop, detain, or arrest; the constitutional rights you have at that very moment starts and stops with "You have a right to remain silent."

That means you will need a lawyer which may be free or not. But be aware that the lawyer, as practicing legal practitioner, cannot mediate your impending detention and or arrest without going before the judge on your behalf.

Here is your smartest and critical assurance -obeying any lawful commands given by officers during traffic stops in the first place would not lead to bodily injury, a visit to the hospital for treatment or in a body bag to the coroners ice cold bench. Granted, you might have a bruised ego and some temporary shame from onlookers edging you to take a stand and fight back.

During Police Encounter - Ask yourself these 3 questions

In the case of traffic stops, officers are taught to observe drivers either visually or by the use of radars - (Radio Detection and Ranging) which uses electromagnetic waves, the officer or officers of the law would immediately activate the siren and the blue lights. Of course, depending on your city, state, and local areas; some authorities have red lights mounted on their patrol cars.

Most, if not all police vehicles have audio communications for the patrol officer driving to direct the driver of the vehicle being stopped for alleged infractions to safely stop at a location suitable for both driver and driving officer to safely interact to determine the next course of action as prescribed by the law. And today, most if not all law enforcement vehicles are equipped with video cameras to observe traffic movement and unusual events on the roads.

The initial non-verbal command from the law enforcement officer driving the clearly marked police vehicle would be the signal for you to pull away safely from moving traffic and stop for face-to-face interaction. Following this non-verbal siren and flashing lights behind your vehicle, you must directly become responsive to the command by the officer to stop. This simple command to stop and obey the law as it is written does not mean you are lower than, and it does not mean you are a bad person nor target you as a criminal. The law is for every driver on every roadway across the nation and state.

During Police Encounter - Ask yourself these 3 questions

And in all cases, you have to conclude in your mind that the officer is acting in good faith at least until you obey the command to stop. This would be the beginning of a commonsense decision not to escalate a mere traffic stop into a deadly roadside confrontation.

Failure to obey the initial non-verbal command to stop will require the driving officer to activate the microphone in the patrol car to direct the driver to pull over. Again, not applying common sense, by refusing to obey this simple command to reasonably come to a safe stop; would turn what was an ordinary traffic stop which could have lasted no more than twenty to thirty minutes with simple compliance, could now be escalated to a do or die outcome potentially jeopardizing your life and many other families life on the road when it becomes a police chase.

This unwise decision by some, not to pullover and safely come to a successful stop is the beginning of an escalation to some of the sad news surrounding simple traffic stops for minor infractions anywhere in the United States. And it raises the officer's antenna that there is possibility a crime has occurred or that he or she has discovered a potential crime in progress. And because the driver refused to stop, it gives the incentive to the officer to find out exactly what is actually going on.

Other factors likely to surface during a traffic stop could involve but not limited to instances where a driver has had an unresolved prior encounter or encounters with other law-enforcements in the current

During Police Encounter - Ask yourself these 3 questions

jurisdictions or elsewhere that include outstanding warrants, suspended driving privileges, operating motor vehicle under the influence of an illegal substance, or just as simple as anti-police sentiments or the perception of racism and frustrations link to police brutality allegations within various groups.

Whatever the reasons, fleeing law enforcement officers poses more danger than just trying to get away.

1. First, it is one hundred percent certain that no one ever gets away from police chase. Few things would happen. You will be arrested in the end but most definitely battered up, you may end up being severely injured, you may also cause another person or persons to lose their lives prematurely, or worst yet; you may lose your life.
2. It only adds more than the initial reason you are trying to flee from. Means, once the chase is ended by all means necessary, you will most definitely go away to jail and when it is finally resolved, you are more likely to go to prison than not. All for not willing to stop and have a conversation about whatever it was.
3. It is a danger trap for innocent families on the highway when a driver refuses to stop forcing pursuing law enforcement officers to have to resolve to use PIT Maneuvers (Precision Immobilization Technique), a tactical driving maneuver seldom

During Police Encounter - Ask yourself these 3 questions

employed unless a driver refuses to employ his or her common sense.)

4. Running or not running from traffic stops comes back to the application of common sense again! With regular law-abiding drivers on our roads and highways just minding their business, law enforcement officers are the only entity authorized to make arrests and transport law breakers to downtown or wherever the police station is located.
5. Police officers, in essence; are the undisputed king of the roads for peace loving drivers. And stopping to obey the issued commands is one indirect way that smart drivers acknowledge that officers in patrol cars are king of the roads regardless of what they look like or what grievances we have from previous experiences. It is all about that very moment you are being stopped, not last night, last week, last year or last century.

There are no nationwide police records or FBI statistics on total number of deaths due to driver's refusal to simply obey the law. In the hundreds or thousands annually as chases occur daily across the nation and the internet is full of chases particularly in California where lax laws indirectly encourage drivers to comply if they desire.

Remember that it is not the fastest car on the road that is king of the road. There is no other place where the evidence of "You can run, but

During Police Encounter - Ask yourself these 3 questions

you cannot hide" [8] more visible than a driver trying to elude a police officer anywhere in the United States. This quote simply means you can try to escape what you fear most but ultimately you must face it. And it is attributed to the 1940's great heavyweight boxing Champion Joe Louis aka the Bronx Bomber, in an impending fight with the then light heavy weight champion named Billy Conn.

Fleeing or obeying command to pull over for traffic stops comes back to the application of common sense again! With regular law-abiding drivers on our roads and highways just minding their business, law enforcement officers are the only entity authorized to make arrests and transport law breakers to downtown or wherever the police station is located.

Police officers, in essence; are the undisputed king of the roads for peace loving drivers. And stopping to obey the issued commands is one indirect way that smart drivers acknowledge that officers in patrol cars are king of the roads regardless of what they look like or what grievances we have from previous experiences. It is all about now, not last week, last year or last century.

The officer has the right to stop anyone and provide you with a reason you were stopped. Full evidence of that stop would be provided to the courts much later on the appointed date on your citation. Body cameras

[8] https://www.peregrineprivatecapital.com/dsts-you-can-run-but-you-cant-hide/

During Police Encounter - Ask yourself these 3 questions

worn by officers will speak for you if the officer tries to overlook or cover up any of the interaction, or attempts to exaggerate your input during the stop. With all of this, why won't you stop for a brief moment so that you can be on your way to wherever you were heading.

No amount of fuss, argument, or even intimidation on your part would change that date and time. It is then up to you to show up to defend yourself with or without a lawyer if you are feeling like a winner. Not showing up for the court assigned date and time is another level of failure to exercise common sense.

Law enforcement officers are easy to identify by their uniforms and other accessories. Granted, there are some who might choose to impersonate an officer to enable the commission of a crime. For genuine law enforcement officers, you are likely to encounter, they have many tools of trade which you and I fully paid for to make their dangerous job easy to do. Start from the clearly marked vehicles that bear the insignia of the district of its origin.

For instance, an Atlanta Police vehicle would have the city's name, precinct of which the vehicle and the officer driving it was dispatched from, so is a small-town police car in rural South Florida or Nevada. When you see the car, you will know the locality of its origin. Each police vehicle also has some numbers written on its side usually on the driver side rear for easy identification for anyone who cares to look.

During Police Encounter - Ask yourself these 3 questions

In a traffic stop, you can make mental notes of such number, if necessary, usually three to four numbers. In Georgia and some other states, GV, on the government license plates stands for Government. It's best to know these minor things for many reasons. All vehicles bearing GV license plates are government vehicles, but not all are law enforcement officers.

Each officer has a badge and badge number to help identify the officer during contact with citizens. The badge is just as powerful in community policing as any other items such as the vehicles they drive, police service weapons, handcuffs, pepper spray, police radio and booklets you normally would not notice unless you are receiving a citation.

The citation you receive is your invitation to appear before the judge as charged and alleged by the officer at the scene of the incident and or accident. It has date and time. 'This is nothing you just go home and forget about it.' It is nothing you put in your back pocket and realize it has gotten lost and you decide, oh well! You do not want to miss a court date. Missing a court date is the next worst thing to fleeing from police when asked to stop.

Here is an analogy for you to know the very seriousness of this minor thing in your mind. It is like committing a murder, and leaving not only your DNA, but your drivers' license and your cellphone behind which would allow investigators to find you before you could get rid of the murder weapon. Do not miss your court date. Because once the court session is over, the bailiff would already issue that arrest warrant for you.

And let us pray that you were not planning to get married the day you were found or planning to travel outside of the country or city. Consider all plans grounded because of failure to show for your scheduled hearing. Also, remember that you can always call in to get an extension for any reasonable excuses. The court is likely to grant you at least one extension for continuance if you ask. But it has to be done before the court date, or it would certainly be denied as the calendar is usually filled in days before the actual date.

The citation you will receive for any type of traffic offense which is likely to be a misdemeanor, will be stipulated in your written summons. Most misdemeanor traffic offenses provide you the option to pay online without coming to court if you are pleading guilty or nolo contendere. Unless of course you have become antagonistic and combative during the stop at which the officer can mandate your presence before the judge.

And if the obvious unruly behavior interpreted by the officer as excessive, disrespectful, and non-cooperative, he or she may call for backup and haul you away to jail. Then you ask, is that really fair? Well, does it rain in Southern California? It is about the decision you made.

During Police Encounter - Ask yourself these 3 questions

No one, I mean no one; not even the sixteen-year-old working in McDonald's would take excessive abuse from anyone pretending to be holier than thou. Try going into the bank and commence to yelling and fussing at the cashier or just call them a name out of the ordinary. There will be consequences to pay. Law enforcement officers, and even privately owned businesses, and common fast-food restaurants would clap back if you decided to disrespect or abuse their minimum wage employees.

Remember we talked about common sense earlier. It is the primary tool one should employ when dealing with anyone, or any corporate representatives particularly those who are in our presence to serve. not just police officers, but anyone in the position of authority.

During Police Encounter - Ask yourself these 3 questions

CHAPTER 5 **ENJOY YOUR LIFE**

Would you rather take yourself out to the ballpark to enjoy a nice warm summer day for much less than what it would cost you if you were able to suppress your pride for a few minutes. Think about the number of hotdogs, cold ones and peanuts you can have at the Braves Truist Ball Park if you are in Atlanta on a sizzling summer day.

As being disagreeable with the officer is considered obstruction of a law enforcement officer in the execution of his official duty. This type of offense wastes a lot of your hard-earned Benjamins.

Many professional agitators on local and their superior race hustlers on cable television channels indirectly encourage the ruins of many lives. These are the professionals who will have too loaded firearms, give you one, and they too would have one. They would persuade you via many techniques by constant barrage of 'that person is evil, we are on your side, we must fight back, he has no right to stop you and much more.

Really? Of course he has the right to stop you. That was his job description. Observe something out of place, and investigate. There cannot be an investigation without interaction during traffic incidents. And it just so happen to be your turn. Tomorrow, it may be your neighbor. Fill you up with anger and watch you spiral into recklessness.

Once you are filled with rage, it is time to act. Remember those two loaded weapons? They are still there and ready for action. Except you

During Police Encounter - Ask yourself these 3 questions

will have to go first. Not simultaneously, nope. It is you who would fire first into your anatomy, then the demon would do likewise. Do you believe that? I have heard of the Brooklyn Bridge, in fact; I have driven over the Brooklyn Bridge and learnt it is up for sale. Except this time, I am giving it to you free if you believe the lies the enemy of your progress who is pretending to be your friend. Bro, things might be hard for now, but it will only get better if you change who you listen to and who influences your life. None of those who urge on to think certain ways would pay your bills once in 2026.

Like they say, when the rubber meets the road. Have you thought about the meaning of the phrase – here again- "When the rubber meets the road" simply means putting the theory or the ideas of which is the selling point for those encouraging to thoroughly ruin you only one life when theirs, their offsprings are having incredible achievements after another. When you put their words into action, it is where the rubber meets the road.

Naturally, all you will get in return for your troubles are just empty words and rhetoric. What do you think?

On numerous occasions over the last forty-to-fifty years, I have simply driven away with verbal warnings because the officer did not perceive me as a threat or an ignorant fool. And you are too my brother; you are certainly not one. You are royal and as your mother would say, "You know better than that son." While the agitators would agitate, you mother elevates. She would guide you towards your goals. You will make it but first, start enjoying your life. One day at a time.

Many professional agitators on local and cable television channels indirectly encourage without any moral clarity that citizens should know their rights when it comes to police officers conducting traffic stops. Well, when was the last time you turn on the idiot box and see anyone of those fussing and arguing with police officers during traffic stops? Never! Why? Because they are smart enough not to use the very same advice they push to you twenty-four-seven, three-sixty-five. They are more compliant than a five-year-old with hands caught in a cookie jar.

Unfortunately, the television professional agitators that encourage you to know and fight for your constitutional rights are privately avoiding saying many positive things about the constitution publicly except when it is used to rattle you into anger on the roadside. And too many young men have met an untimely death attempting to litigate their rights in a traffic stop instead of the courtroom.

Perhaps check to see how many of these people came to visit the mother of the last victim of their hateful rhetoric powered by ideology and much more but without an iota of care or love for the departed individual. May this not be your portion. It sounds intelligent that a gathering mob would encourage you to fight the law to prove manhood. Having the crowd cheering you on may feel like a useful tool to have in the woke toolbox, but once you use this knowledge tool, it

During Police Encounter - Ask yourself these 3 questions

drives you further away from your primary goals of living your life to the fullest. As a driver, do not be deceive by taking matters into your own hands no matter how angry you are with the face you see at your car door when you are pulled over for any reason at all.

Let me say that one more time – when you are pull over for any reason's at all, do not consider the face you see at your car door the enemy. Remember that about 50,000 [9] drivers are pulled over in the United States of America daily, and you are just one of them. For you, you are just in the wrong place, at the right time. For the officer who is just doing his professional job, you are like every day for the thief, it is only one day for the owner.

Majority of drivers might be speeding at the time you were stopped, but the RaDar (Radio Detection and Ranging) has locked in on you when it is properly calibrated which is often is.

Realistically, 49,999 drivers stopped for traffic offense would go home to eat supper that very same day and not end up in the mortuary. Mostly, none would end up on the evening news or with loud and agitated crowd gathering to further enflamed the situation to your detriment. The one out of many that may not go home that night may have had an unfulfilled obligation causing the judicial system to issue a

[9] Google AI - How many drivers are pulled over for traffic citations on a daily basis in the US?

During Police Encounter - Ask yourself these 3 questions

warrant of arrest for such person.

This in its face value, is not a dead sentence. Like any challenges or problems, it can properly be resolved. Also, the resolution can serve as a life's lesson that may help such person to avoid such future occurrences. The result would be a lesson's learned.

Can you just imagine why it is that one out of 50,000 people stopped for potential traffic violations might not go home after the encounter with the exception of prior warrants issued by the courts. It will be because the most common tools for successful human interactions were not properly deployed during the exchange with the officer on site . And that is something we called "common sense." More about common sense and its useful application much later in this project. Like most men, when they are in a pickle; we tend to call for our mother. As well as when we are in the limelight of professional sports. Chants of "Hi Mom" is the most common thing you will hear during broadcasts of college and professional sports.

During Police Encounter - Ask yourself these 3 questions

CHAPTER 6 **SIMPLY COMPLY**

Whenever a police traffic stop occurred, how nice would it be to hear from a reasonable mother that will say, "you know better son, give that man your driver's license and you'll soon be on your way home." Instead of those looking to edge you on towards failure.

In any traffic stop, once the driver obeys the command to safely pull over and stop would be, "Driver's license please." Most officers without any aggravating circumstances upon complete stoppage of the motor vehicle, which includes shutting the engine off, having your hands where the officer or officers can clearly observe them would be, Driver's license please. Again, hand it over.

The primary reason you have a driver's license is for the law to be able to identify you when you are making contact. Remember I said, "primary reason?" Yes, that is the primary reason for having a driver's license issued by the state. Other usefulness for the driver's license is just bi-product of having it. Like using it to cash a check at the local grocery stores, identifying yourself at the local nightclub so they know you are of legal age.

Come to think of it, have you ever refused to just hand over your driver's at anywhere if you are asked? Particularly if you want to finalize any business dealings. So, think! Why would you refuse to give an officer of the state your driver's license? I think some of the

During Police Encounter - Ask yourself these 3 questions

programming starts with talking head non lawyers who really have no degree in anything than creating disunity among brethren. The police are not your enemy by all means.

Again, the demand to give your license is not a suggestion, it is a command and the command does not mean you are lower than. It is not an opportunity for you to argue, to challenge, or to belittling the officer for what you perceived is wrongful interruption of your leisurely ride. Everyone who is pulled over has a sincere obligation to produce their driver's license. Period!

If by chance you forgot it at home, politely explain to the officer. If it was lost, politely informed the officer. If it has been suspended and you're aware, it is still okay. This will not cause a loss of life.

Tell the officer and wait for the next instructions. If it had been suspended but you were not aware, the officer will know and tell you what to do next. This is not a life-threatening circumstance. If you are not licensed to drive, prepare to go to jail. It is not the end of your driving life.

Step out of the car please: Simply obey this simple instruction. It is for your safety and the officer or officer's safety. Obey! After you have obeyed the instructions to step out of the car, a few things will happen, your reasonable job is to continue to obey, or if it will make you feel better – simply comply. Police officers are not going get into an

During Police Encounter - Ask yourself these 3 questions

extended conversation with you on the road. It is best if you know this and get used to the simple short phrases you might hear.

You might hear:

a. Your driver's license and registration please.
b. Seat in your car, I will be right back.
c. Step out of the car please.
d. You are under arrest for (and the type of violation or violations will be read out to you expressly.)
e. Put your hands behind your back. It is unlikely that your Miranda rights will be read to you for traffic violations on the side of the road except there was a pending warrant(s) for your arrest for prior infractions and or violations.
f. And also, if there was a need to question you about the arrest at some point, then a Miranda is warranted to ensure your given statement is admissible before the trial court. Depending on the level of your infractions, violations, and your cooperations, you might hear the officer call for back-up. This is sometimes necessary during an arrest. Again, it is for your safety and security as well as for the arresting officer(s).

During Police Encounter - Ask yourself these 3 questions

Strive forward to let people see your royalty when they see you and not just your color at your lowest point. Imagine what could go right when you see the blue lights and hear the sirens. Just imagine for a minute. You pull over with your blinking lights indicating you are complying with the officer's directives. For me, I know what I usually do. I remove my wallet, remove my license and have it in hand by the time the officer approaches my window.

One last thing I do also is to lower my window so as to allow the officer to see who else is in the car and if there is nobody but me.

You goal is not to heighten the intensity of a traffic stop; you goal is to go home to your loved ones. Period! Let some macho guys without a goal to live a decent life do that. That is certainly not you. When he shows up, I say greetings like "good evening or good afternoon officer." By addressing him as such, I have shown my humanity.

What you do to lower the temperature is on you. Let it be in line with your priorities and the honor of your family name. If you are a student, then act like that – a student learning to become successful in life would not want to dare to throw it all away for instant with strangers voice being the last thing they will hear saying all sort of things fit for the asylum.

With your co-operations, regardless of what the officer or officers alleged in the citation prepared for you; except for prior failure to

During Police Encounter - Ask yourself these 3 questions

appear in a court of law for hearing or impending warrants for your arrest which you might be aware or not, you are likely to be transported to county or city jail, with the high likelihood that once bond is set and you posted the bond, you may be able go home under (24) twenty four hours with a notice for you to appear in court or you may be schedule for a hearing soon if your bond request is denied high enough that you cannot make.

In the event that you decided to fight or flight, consider that decision as an attempt to endanger your life, the officer(s) lives, and the lives of the general public. And remember that you have not made that decision with the require common sense needed to survive an ordinary traffic stops. And imagine this happened and one of the fatalities is a relative of yours who just happened to be in the wrong place at the right time. That burden on your heart would be heavy for life!

The difference between the two scenarios is humongous. But it is still very minut. The way you think. The way you act. Your thought processes. And before that point, the people you listened to for guidance and influence over your life that has driven your thought process into the negative. Just always remember that when it is all said and done, you will be all alone without a soul that genuinely care.

Whenever you look back and see the blue lights flashing, it is not the end of your life or of the world. It is just a tiny moment that shall pass as well as many others that have in the past. Do you remember what

During Police Encounter - Ask yourself these 3 questions

happened to you on July 17th of last year? How bad was it? It is why history is written. And those negative histories in our lives have been relegated to the dustbin with no value at all. You just keep on keeping home and hoping and praying for the best days to come.

The negative information that has built up in your heart towards any duly commission enforcement officer should not come into play at this very trying moment of your beautiful life. And if and when it does, you have to be prepared to assume the responsibilities that come with that decision. The officer has nothing to do with your voluntary actions behind the wheel.

However; employing an irrational thought process, deploying a sense of pride and arrogance, and a pure decision to litigate your rights at a traffic stop could suddenly put your overall well-being at great danger. At the end of the day, the outcome, whether good or bad, worse of fatal; only you and your loved ones would suffer all the consequences. Oh, the officer will too.

If you failed to co-operate, your actions might negatively impact the officer. It may even cost him or her his or her life. So, what is the prize of this negative outcome? The first prize belongs to many families on both sides. The pain and the suffering of grandparents, parents, spouses, children, uncles and aunts, cousins, nephews, and nieces, loved animals like dogs and cats, co-workers, classmates and even your nosey neighbors.

During Police Encounter - Ask yourself these 3 questions

You can even add your love for the vehicle you were driving when you encounter the officer. You may not be able to drive that beautiful car for a while or ever. All of that for a quick second reaction to bruised egos. Such negative actions would invalidate your primary goals set when you left home that day.

And that is to fulfil all of the things you said before you stepped out: "see you later," "talk to you later after class," "I'll be right back." This one encounter at a traffic stop is not worth making later a permanent end to a life's story.

The fight to justify that your civil and human rights might have been violated, and in most instances that might be the case, however; the need to vindicate your esteem self at the perceived offense or offender(s), and your desire to dominate, retaliate and humiliate the perpetrator of such crime of possible disrespect or even civil rights violations, let me let you know that victory for such attempt to vindicate yourself on the side of the road would not be won. It will even cost you more frustration, time, and more Benjamins.

Why? Because it is not favorable to your physical, financial, and mental wellbeing to pick a fight with an officer of the law as long as America is not back to Wild, Wild, West! At times, it may be tempting if you are six feet two, weighing in at two hundred and sixty-five pounds and the officer is ninety-five pounds female. Traffic enforcement on America's roads is not by might. Even if you are physically superior to the

During Police Encounter - Ask yourself these 3 questions

officer(s), you still have to obey when common sense is applied one hundred percent of the time.

Remember your primary goal, in fact your ultimate goal when you left your place of dwelling or employment, or any other starting point is what? To safely return back to your loved ones and finish all of the unfinished business.

When there is conflict that results in physical altercation, even if you are justified; and even if it is with another ordinary citizen, and it requires the presence of law enforcement; your inalienable rights as a law-abiding citizen have just been downgraded from a potential written summons when handled properly to a citizen that might be accused of a crime and haul off to jail. And if it is between you and a designated law enforcement officer; remember that you cannot issue summons, he or she can! At the stroke of a written summons, your freedom, as bad as it sounds; is temporarily restricted effective immediately. It's Super Bowl Sunday and you are having friends over. Nope! You are heading straight to jail.

This is an inconvenient situation when sometimes pride, built-in angst, and past historical conflicts is activated. Conflict resolution is best resolved at the proper place, not on the side of the road particularly when one person -you- has decided that there is no hierarchy at this point. The recipe prescribes in this book gives you the best shot at winning not the poison pills pushed incessantly by total strangers.

During Police Encounter - Ask yourself these 3 questions

Like in anything else in life, officer-driver relationships fall under an order of hierarchy. You might argue with a barber, a salesperson, or your auto mechanic; but to be truthful; I will dare you to argue with a judge with his robe on sitting on the bench without detrimental, severe, regrettable consequences.

This is the highest order on the hierarchy encounters that start on the roadside. And mind you, the judge does not carry a weapon, nor does it always stand strong and tall. It is only common sense that dictates that this person with the title of a judge has been fully empowered to pass judgments on anyone attending the courtroom by summons or as an ordinary observe if there was some unbecoming actions or even re-actions. And it's still the same common sense that says, "Be at your best behavior" even if you're right by perception.

In contrast, police officers have the same mandate. To haul you away for any and all offenses against persons, property, and governmental entities. The difference is that the judge sits in his or her courtroom and waits for you to show up based upon the summons given to you informing you to appear in court.

Police officers whether in uniforms or undercover officers on the other hand are authorized to carry guns, badges, handcuffs, and automobile for transportation and as transport motor vehicles for offenders. So, if you wouldn't argue with a weaponless judge, while would you risk going to war with a duly authorized officer with power to- be it right or wrong- employ deadly; justifiable force when necessary.

But remember, a dead man or woman cannot experience the satisfaction of a wrongful death decision in any courtroom.

Levels of Authority on our roadways - Static Traffic Signs, Video monitoring visuals, School environment peace officers, Speed monitoring technologies, Police cars equipped with Lights & Sirens, Motorcycles equipped with Lights & Sirens, law enforcement officer's tools of enforcement which includes Uniforms, Badges, Guns, Handcuffs and automobiles that provide free rides to a designated reception area for non-compliant, accused suspects, the Courts include Clerks, Bailiffs, Sheriffs, and ultimately, the Judge.

Which one of these elements of justice do you believe you can argue with without incurring severe consequences? Only a true fool would go to the courthouse and decide to argue with the sitting judge. The person behind the robe may not be a god, but he or she is not ordinary either. Regardless of which authorities you are in these United States, the power of a judge can reach out and touch you when it is warranted.

As the Bible commands us to respect and honor our fathers and our mothers, yet; some finds a way to circumvent that godly command by taking it for granted; in the courtroom, it is the law of State that commands each person doing business with the courts to respect and honor the judge, and the entire court personnels to include the bailiff,

During Police Encounter - Ask yourself these 3 questions

court clerk, recorder, and everyone at various windows collecting fines and court assessed fees.

Now, if one is not reckless enough to disobey or disrespect a sitting judge on the bench, why then should one decide to disobey or disrespect law enforcement officers with the authority to use deadly force? It comes down to the matter of vital common sense. So, once again, let's revisit AI for one of the reasons why common sense is vital:

"It helps you evaluate situations and consequences to make good choices, rather than impulsive or foolish ones." In the case of each person's interaction with the law enforcement communities, common sense helps us to understand that each officer is like the entire town, city, county, and state. No one individual is strong enough to challenge the authority designated by these localities to each officer as they go about enforcing the laws set by various elected officials of each town, city, county, and state.

If at the end of the traffic stop, you failed to win the argument no matter how long the officer(s) allowed it to continue; you will now make a trip to the dreaded downtown. This is the scene from the movie where you wanted to be pinched as if this was all but a confused dream. Your car has been impounded. Your possessions on hand before the incident now are confiscated items that will be booked alongside you.

During Police Encounter - Ask yourself these 3 questions

Your phones, wallet, and just pray that you do not have any contraband on your person that will surely lead to extra charges against you. Can you feel it now?

Now the dust has settled, by all means necessary; you are finally arrested, cuffed, placed in the back of the police squad car; not a single agitator would volunteer to go in your stead to jail for that day. Not one, not any. No matter how hard they have shouted and lounge obscenities at the officers for doing their job.

Somebody might have yelled racism. Ask yourself, were you really stopped become of your race? If that is the case, what would a white person stopped by a law enforcement officer says? All the unreasonable fuels added to inflame your anger and get you feeling you must do something! Now, it is you alone sitting in the back of the squad car hungry, tired, and even sleepy. The ego that boosted and fueled with racism is deflated and the crowd has moved on to another event.

It is like a shot of hot whiskey on an empty stomach. It would just be you and your maker wondering what is next. Once you arrive at the station to be booked, no doubt your eyes will come down, and the effect of the noise of fake supporters will disappear as if you have just had a bad dream. Naturally, you will as for a phone call. Who will it be? Mom? Lawyer? Spouse if you have one Or one of those agitators who has taken the video of your arrest and began to monetize it on the web. Who will it be? You might call your lovely mother if you are blessed to

During Police Encounter - Ask yourself these 3 questions

have one available.

And it is you, and only you that can determine your next. stop after encountering law enforcement officers in what should be an unremarkable exchange between you and the officer whose role is to serve and to protect.

Take your mind back to the very first moment you were pulled over. Could you have done something differently? Like, "hello officer." And initially, you might hear "your driver's license and registration please." Even if both you and the officer decided not to exchange platitudes, you can still simply comply with the officer(s) directives.

Your pride, ego, your itching to tell him off would still be there when your concluded your casual interactions and both of you would be on your merry ways. You will continue, and the officer would also continue either to the next driver or to his or her own family. I will see you in court. It would sound so great if the bye for now is mutual.

Your interaction with the officer(s) at the scene should be simple. Simple only if you are willing to listen to him as someone authorized to conduct a traffic stop; therefore, the officer(s) was conducting his or her legitimate task. So far, so good. Unless there is an animosity towards a total stranger, in most cases; someone you might have never seen before. And if not, then you should show the same respect you will show to a sitting judge if you are to be in his or her courtroom.

During Police Encounter - Ask yourself these 3 questions

As the officer is part of that judicial system.

And if you receive a citation, you will end up going to sit in a courtroom to face the judge. The word "Authority" is defined by Thesaurus dictionary as "the power or right to give orders, make decisions, and enforce obedience." This definition is all one needs to know about the power given by society to law enforcement officials. The power that is given is literal, not subjective nor metaphorically speaking but concrete and absolute unless when abused.

And when abused, resolution cannot be found on the roadside. The attempt to obtain justice on roadside and highways almost resulted in bigger catastrophe than one is attempting to solve. Financial catastrophe is the least of the numerous pains litigating one's right by the roadside would bring. Not could, but would bring. Let us start with the potential for physical catastrophe, mental catastrophe, bondage catastrophe, and the ultimate is the loss of one's life which is the end of all things we all hold dearly.

And this catastrophe is the burden that loved ones would surfer for years to come. Particularly on your birthday, your anniversary if you are married, the date the catastrophic incident happened, thanksgiving, Christmas, amongst others. So, ask yourself if the prize of instant vindication on the roadside is much more valuable to you than all you could lose fighting rather than a simple compliance for no more than 30 minutes delay. And you will still live with your pride intact.

During Police Encounter - Ask yourself these 3 questions

No one is above the law is a phrase that certain office holders have been throwing around over the last few years. There is no venue that this phrase is more true than during a traffic stop. Judges, when violating city, state, or federal ordinances are often ticketed like any other citizens. When a judge is belligerent and acting in a way that attempts to usurp the officer's power to issue a citation, the judge can face reprimand, and in some cases of drunk driving, can face the possibility of disbarment. And such judge can be charged with "abuse of power."

"Abuse of Power is when a judge act entitled or uses their badge to intimidate an officer, it's a serious issue, as seen with Judge Dennis Reinaker, who was reprimanded for telling an officer to check his own registration." [10]

As we can see here in the above paragraph, a judge who challenged an officer of the law in the course of performing official duties was duly punished by the system. Considering the relationship between the officer and the judge is that of a superior official in higher level versus a very junior member of the law enforcement division. However, while the officer is working the designate beat; as in patrol vehicle, the judge must recognize the role reversal between the two.

---

[10] Google AI- Do judges get stopped while driving for infractions?

During Police Encounter - Ask yourself these 3 questions

While on patrol, for a brief shining moment; the officer is chief amongst equals while still affording cordial respect for all traffic encounters irrespective of their professional titles vis-à-vis judge, janitor, or journalist. In this example, we see a role reversal based on the appropriate settings. The same police officer may be assigned to the same judge tomorrow for various details, the officer would also understand the role for that occasion which is only subject to change when he or she is back in a position of authority in a patrol car and or work environments where the judge has no control.

For an honorable law enforcement officer operating behind the patrol vehicles either from observatory point or driving about, he or she has authority and no doubt superior to every citizen regardless of status or official duties particularly as it relates to operating a motor vehicle on any public roads or highways. This armed body of the government is designated as entity responsible for facilitating link between the society, justice and punishment. They are charged by all of us to help bring about accountability from those who will choose not voluntarily complied with societal norms.

And it is up to each of us to decide which side we choose to operate. that chose to sit behind the wheel and drive or even parked on a public street, businesses, or local, state, and federal highways. You encounter with any officer is, and should not become an exercise in futility where the officer is regarded as your enemy because of prior racial animus.

During Police Encounter - Ask yourself these 3 questions

CHAPTER 7. PROFESSIONAL GANGSTERS

This is about professional gangsters. Not the gang you know and fear, but the one you listen to daily for the directions your very own heart should go. These gangsters are potent. They might be next to you right now and you may not know it. You wake up listening to some of them and when you retired to bed at night; you are likely to get your marching orders. Soon, you will see that you too are a very discreet gang member.

But it is not too late to get your freedom and take full control of your thought process and bid adieu to the gang handlers finally. This world is full of gangs. Yes, gangs. But the gangs that are most talked about are obviously visible gangs because of their propensity to hurt people physically as well as their ability to organize solely to disrupt, enforce and enforced a structured code of behavior amongst its members.

These scrupulous gangs are known very well because of the damages they have caused to human lives, families that they have ruined, high school student they recruited who once has a full potential to become somebody and was soon wasted either by gang violence or by using illicit drugs. The drug gangsters have distributed drugs in the inner city and even have customers who come from the affluent suburbs.

So, yes; they deserve their notoriety for causing economic destruction, in some cases; entire city such as Gary, Indiana, West side Chicago,

During Police Encounter - Ask yourself these 3 questions

Detroit, Michigan; Compton, California; and many cities too numerous to mention. Cities where houses has been abandoned and residents moved out of town for the sake of their young children's lives. Once prominent neighborhoods have been abandoned and the homes their turned into alleyways for illicit transactions to include drugs and often prostitutions.

It is clear why many have such disdain for the notorious gangsters in their communities. Most gangs are known by their tattoos, the colors they wear, and the specific crimes they are organized to perpetrate on innocent victims. If you were to try to attach collar to these types of gangs and gangsters; they would have no collar at all.

In the past, gangs are limited to just men. Strong men who are willing to take risks and even kill their family members if the need arises to prove their loyalty to the gang leaders. Today, it's quite common to have a gang of men and women working cohesively to disrupt lives of others. Some gangs are even operating within the school systems where it is easy to recruit many confused young people who felt neglected at home or by their caretakers. Also, there are gangs within the prison systems.

And membership in the prison gang group is often for survival reasons. You need protection, then you must join a particular unit otherwise you risk serious bodily injuries. All gangs have membership oath to declare their truthful allegiance to the group which is a code of honor

During Police Encounter - Ask yourself these 3 questions

administer during the initiation process. Breaking the oath or even a mere violations or betrayal of the trust could cost the member his or her life. So, when someone talk about gangs, these are the thought that came to mind.

But wait, there are other types of gangs with no membership affiliations, no oaths to be taken, no monthly dues, no clearly marked identification numbers, no color orientations, and definitely no initiation process. The professional gangster handlers wears suit, pant-suit, sometimes skirt and blouse but never the do-rag (also known as bandana) that the no-collar gang dress code many are familiar with when featured on the evening news. These gang handlers are well dressed and with such appearance; many are fooled into believing every lies they tell, every agenda they push, and every target they selected for destruction.

Gang members get their fix from the professional gang handlers through an open ideological means. Members are completely brainwashed to focus their energy on a specific target and battle internally about all the wrong things that the alleged target has caused them in immeasurable ways. And as bad as it gets; members pay monthly fees to each medium to receive this marching orders.

I remember about ten years ago; my cable carrier informed me that my feed was going to increase significantly and if I chose not to pay the extra increase, my daily hate-spewing handler and her associates will be

During Police Encounter - Ask yourself these 3 questions

dropped from my subscription package. I could not let that happened. So, I raise Cain, and when Cain refused to rise, I succumb to the pressure and pony off more money to keep that one captive handler within arm's length.

I could not afford to miss all of the instructions, tit-bits, and yes lies about a target who has not offended me and yet I am supposed to hate as if my life depends upon it. The power of constant barrage of lies has firmly gripped my mind. But for God and God only that did not allow my mind to wonder too far off. It is like someone saying something about my mother. Jeepers Creepers!

Deliberately, without being forced or coerce, I voluntarily paid my hard earn money to invite detractors into my home. That means if you have television in your home, you are also a gangster with or without your permission. The worst part about this in-house presence is that it can summarily turn a peaceful home to a battleground.

The potency of the handlers venom, once it is spewed into your living or bedroom through the idiot box, your peaceful home now has an enemy present, and it is subject to occasional volcanic activities. This is likely to happen when two happily married couples have two separate set of believes when it comes to ideology. But mind you, couples have been able to talk over their ideological difference for decades in this country. Now, fungus amongst us has thrown numerous kakafu into many family's peaceful home with constant drumbeat that anyone who

During Police Encounter - Ask yourself these 3 questions

disagreed with you should be made into a pariah, isolated and considered as 'other.' This is un-American! Nothing like this has ever been seen in this land. I do not believe that anyone, any group, any organization, or any handler would be this committed to a cause without an underpinning benefits. Benefits which superseded in-born loyalties to these United States. I may be wrong however; I doubt it!

The gangs use various mouthpiece to keep you engaged. Your primary obligation is to hate. And the target of your hate is not of your own choosing. Not because the target has offended you directly or even indirectly. But once the order is given, and your heart is tapped into with subliminal messages, you are activated for self-destruction.

You are wandering how do I know all of these secrets about the professional gangsters and their ability to pit family against family in the name of some kind of ideology? Well, I was once a member. I was so excited that I would take all my money just to be able to go to any event where like-minded people were gathering locally and sometimes outside of my residing state.

There are several levels of unaffiliated leadership structures in this particular gang structure. One of the most effective unaffiliated leadership structure that captured my mind for twelve years is a certain propaganda handlers with ten to twelve hours devoted to keeping the gang members fed. Giving the people what they want.

During Police Encounter - Ask yourself these 3 questions

They are extremely well rehearsed. Nothing is real or genuine in their presentations and they knew it.

The most important thing to them is the clients, the gang members, and the addicts like me did not fully understand their intentions until it has consumed me to become so hateful towards someone I have never met in my life. We were not programmed as captives to think. That is absolutely forbidden. Our handlers think for us. Just like zombies, they say go, and we go.

There was no weapons issued by the gang handlers. Weapons are not necessary. They just captured your mind and that in itself is more powerful than a bazooka. Membership is this operation that turns you into a Zombie waiting for your daily orders. I spent those twelve years wanting for more. And for no reasons that I can explain I wanted it morning, noon and night. I became dependent on my five pm fix, six pm fix, seven pm fix, 8 pm fix, 9 pm fix was extremely toxic and at the same time intoxicating. My handler came ready to spew venoms like an aggravated viper. Boy, do I take it all in? Yes I did! I ate it as if it was apple pie. I never got enough of the poisonous diet.

They were relentless to the point that I could barely sleep as I waited to get my morning dose of whatever they have as the new outrage of the day. In the meanwhile; I found out that I was spending in excess of eight to ten hours daily watching these propagandists, a bad habit that might later give one hypertension if not properly diagnose and cure.

During Police Encounter - Ask yourself these 3 questions

In the meanwhile; the least paid of these human outrage source were making in the ballpark of four million dollars ($4 million) annually with benefits galore. And I was barely making ends meet like many Americans in the land, I mean in the gang. These guys were like my handlers. I wake up, turn on the idiot box, get my instructions; off to the races. Who is my target for today? Who am I hating on?

"Treat the Truth like Chips, Let Them Fall where They May." [11]

I started wandering if I am actually controlling my political feelings in a democracy that they scream twenty-four-seven. Am I really happy with the ideology shoved at me relentlessly without any benefits? I took another stock in my mind to remind myself that we are in a democracy where it is said to be one man, one vote. Then I realized that my vote was not really my vote.

It belongs to my handlers who instructed me that this person is bad, that group is bad, and that party is bad. And that I must think a certain way without considering my very own mental health. This types of subliminal messages on airwaves should be considered illegal without censorship. At least prevent other people from planting a time bomb into someone's mind like viewers are zombies as in the apocalypse.

---

[11] "Treat the Truth like Chips, Let Them Fall where They May." Jon Moses. From the book "Don't Litigate your rights during police Encounters" Chapter 7 Professional Gangsters.

During Police Encounter - Ask yourself these 3 questions

It has reached a braking point when I evaluates everyone that they say is bad and who they pointed to as good. The light bulbs did not just go off, it blew off. That was my ha-ha moment.

One thing that these handlers would not disclose because no one cares enough to ask is 'who controls their own office environments?' Even the cashier at Burger King would not permit you to come to his or her workplace and dictate terms of conditions. Law enforcement officers primary role is to bring their office to you the consumer. And while the consumer, as a driver has business related circumstances, officers are the primary fixer of all circumstances that is traffic related. And it is best that every customer, either voluntary or happenstance; behave accordingly.

Remember this that while some law enforcement clients might be unhappy, many clients are so happy to see them in times of trouble. For instance, when you get into a fender bender, without that police report written from the summons given to the guilty party, you may have challenges recovering anything. Let us learn to appreciate both in its appropriate times. Listen to your inner self rather than angry agitators, hate mongers, and professional gangsters. Doing so, you will be alright.

CHAPTER 8. **UNDERSTAND THE SYSTEM**

When you are in Rome, it is best to act like Romans. In your home where you live, if you live alone, in so far you pay the rent and mortgage if you own it, then without a doubt; you are the boss of you. When you go to work, no matter what your title is, you might even have a corner office and lots of artificial flowers in your office, as well as you having some employees answering to you every hour of the day, in as long as all things been equal, you are the boss until it is not.

Our society functions so well like a system. If you understand, respect, and know the system, you will know peace. When you failed to treat the system right or pretend that the system is not there, the system is unforgiving. Once you leave your place of dwelling, know that you have relinquished most of your ability to be in charge of anything as soon as you entered the public domain. This is an unspoken rule that all those who studied the system will understand.

I will have to borrow a word I already used in a chapter of this book as it is applicable – common sense. Only those who apply their common sense would know that the system functions best when common sense is applied to every intricate details with regards to the system. The only thing you really have control of is you. And once you have dared to leave your home and venture into public domain, though you still have your rights, however; is it limited. And as an American, it is still second to no other nation on planet earth. That is an undisputed fact.

During Police Encounter - Ask yourself these 3 questions

However; when you try to challenge an authority figure, where the officer is duly commissioned to act of level one enforcer for all of society's troubles, you cannot win that battle.

Imagine some of these locations where you have no authority other than to use and conduct your business and go back to wherever you are heading. Here are some of them: public roads, streets, highways, public parking lots, event centers, malls, public transportation to include air, land and sea, parks, faith-based facilities, learning centers, and yes public library. Do not be fooled by the names public roads and public library.

Some would say, but, but, my tax dollars are used in constructing these projects. The answer is "So what?" What about projects constructed before you started making a dime! And as tax payers, we all have interests in making sure that our laws are enforced without prejudice and favor. All authority; outside of your private residence (assuming that you are not breaking the law behind closed doors) belongs to the Village, City, State and Federal authorities as to the maintenance of law and order.

These are the entities designated by "We The People" and properly equipped to expedite and resolve all activities within the realms of safety and the wellbeing of all members of the society. Of course, we expect that the scale of justice will be balanced for each potential defendant in the court of law. And these are the responsibilities of our

During Police Encounter - Ask yourself these 3 questions

law enforcement officers. It is a monumental task that has the potential to wreak havoc when it is not professionally managed or when it lacks cooperation and support from the community it seeks to protect and serve. Collectively, traffic related incidents is our responsibility to solve however difficult it looks.

In the interim, let us recognize that even as a free country, anything we do outside of our homes deserves some form of authorized guidelines as not all citizens would obey the law of safety and peaceful co-habitation. This failure by some elements within our society crosses the bounds of race, color, ideology, spiritual and nationality. It is of the human element.

During Police Encounter - Ask yourself these 3 questions

CHAPTER 9. **WHY NOT LOVE**

Remember that if you go separate ways after your traffic encounter, and five minutes later something out of the ordinary happens to you, it might be the same officer that will be dispatched to help you out. I have full confidence that he or she would not hesitate to help and neither would you refuse the offer to help you because he or she is white and just recently gave you a citation. Such is the nature of what law enforcement personnel do on a daily basis.

When you get behind the wheels of a motor vehicle, there have to be some supervisory roles for the government that issued you the license to drive on taxpayer funded roads. Otherwise, there would be no license needed to purchase and drive a vehicle of your choice. And most definitely insurance would not be mandated.

License and auto insurance are two major requirements for you to drive. In the absence of regulations, you would not want to drive on our roads for safety reasons. It would be chaotic indeed! And when you apply for these two essentials, you are of the knowledge that with rights comes privileges, and with privileges comes some restrictions for the sake of others. The rights and the privileges are easy to understand. It is the restrictions many have difficulty adjusting to.

Restrictions such as speed limits, automobile insurance to protect other drivers should you cause an accident, also that your automobile must be

During Police Encounter - Ask yourself these 3 questions

road worthy and not a hazard to other drivers on the road as well as understanding the different roads signs. And one more inconvenient that should not be – is handing your driver's license to an officer to confirm you are who you say that you are. Justy comply!

Furthermore, though you determine where you need to go, the government decides what direction you will need to go to get there as well as for you to learn the road signs for your own sake as well as other citizens. The State of Georgia has 20 dedicated road signs. According to Google AI, "The Georgia driver's license knowledge test includes a dedicated 20-question Road Signs section, where you must get at least 15 correct to pass, alongside a Road Rules section, with the entire exam focusing heavily on identifying various signs, signals, and markings, using shapes, colors, and symbols from the official Georgia DDS Driver's Manual." [12]

So, with all of these in the backdrop, your disagreement on the roads with law enforcement officials is a disagreement with all of us. It is why so many who have failed to recognize these simples fact have had to pay a hefty prize. Your disagreement has to be brought to the overseer of the traffic related judicial system, namely the Judge. And that is the appropriate venue for any and all types of litigation. It is the venue where the officer(s) and the accused would have equal representation

---

[12] Georgia DDS Driver's Manual

During Police Encounter - Ask yourself these 3 questions

before the presiding honorable judge.

Would you consider it fair if after you have just humiliated the officer at a traffic stop and you got home and there is a man there attempting to break into your home. What would you first think of doing? Go in there and show the intruder that you are man of great convictions and that you can talk him out of the robbery? Or would you just pick up your phone which is probably so heavy in your pocket by now considering your last encounter was with a police officer you disobeyed his instructions because of bad feelings that translates to "I just don't like police officers no matter what."

Well, let us say that you swallowed your pride in the heat of the moment and grab that heavy phone and dial 9-1-1 and the dispatcher assured you that the officer is on his way. You have now put the officer's life at risk for the second time in less than six hours. Of course it can happen exactly as I described here. Let us say he, because you will not have disrespected a female police officer during your last traffic encounter moments earlier.

He is now speeding to your residence determine to save you from a decrepit burglar armed with some sort of weapon and you do not have one. He pulled up to your place and get out of his patrol car, and you saw him. What now? Shame, remorse, or will you just tell him that I do not like you, and asked him to live now with the same temperaments you exhibited on the road side moments earlier. Knowing how officers

During Police Encounter - Ask yourself these 3 questions

are trained, he will promptly resolve to relieve you of the intruder at the risks to his own well-being. The moral here is the you should learn to show some love to those who put their lives on the line to serve and protect. And yes, there are bad officer like any profession.

By the way, what is your own profession? Are everyone in your profession super decent? Probably not. My brothers and sisters; kindly show some love and let us be kind always even if we are under some external pressures to react negatively to the scapegoats of pollical and ideological bad beats.

When an officer approaches your car, he or she might just be a great guy or gal looking to help. Think about the possibility that the officer who you are in conflict and addressed as racist is married to a person of your own ethnic background with children at home who looks just like you. How painful that would be! 1960's racism versus 2025 racism is as far as the years are far apart - 65apart. Race-ism just might not be the first thing he or she is looking for from a driver stopped for minor traffic infractions. Oh, what IF the officer is a Black person?

Finaly, could you imagine if the officer has just sponsored an American child with her school supplies for the year. I said an American, now add African American child, if that were announced as soon as he approached your vehicle would you smile and say hello? The fact of the matter is you just never know who your friend is based on traffic exchanges. The officer might even show up at your church invited by your pastor, and you never knew Pastor spends time together as in (hanging out) with a responsible human being who is simply different in complexion. Let us learn to accommodate God's angels unaware to receive the peace for which we are desperately searching. Why not Love?

During Police Encounter - Ask yourself these 3 questions

CHAPTER 10. **YOU WIN WHEN YOU DON'T LITIGATE**

I am sure you have heard of a guy named Michael Jordan. He was a professional Basketball Player who most people say that he is the GOAT. GOAT being an acronym for the Greatest Of All Time. I lived in Chicago when Michael was playing for the Bulls. I had a few chance to watch him play at Chicago Center. He was truly as good as they say. But there is one habit of Michael that not so many other players have. Michael does not like to lose.

Not just on the basketball court but playing Golf, playing cards, rolling dice, or name it; he refused to take second. He cares about winning. And you too could be like Mike.

What is your winning strategy? Can you accomplish that goal IF you do not return home today as planned when you left you crib? Would that make you a winner like Mike? If you have to borrow money or use your rent money to post bond because of an encounter with a police officer for traffic related incident, would you consider that a win? What if someone rioting because of you is killed by another Black person? Would the end justify the means? Or you ended up in the hospital in a physically bad shape. Would you consider that a win in your mind?

When you DO NOT LITIGATE YOUR RIGHTS on the roadside against Law ENFORCEMENT OFFICERS(S), you have already won!

During Police Encounter - Ask yourself these 3 questions

And you will live to fight another day in the courtroom with your lawyers by your side and witness(es) if you have any. In my mind right now, I am looking at a famous lawyer who will be the first front and center once you have been involved in an officer related beating or shooting. He stays ready only for those occasions. Unless you are beaten, shot. Or dead; you would not see their likes. Think brother.

Be an outlier in the race related riots and schemes that enrich some and eviscerate others. I am sure you that you belong to others. But the some would push your button until things fall apart. Think! That is not how you win plain and simple. You win by having your day in court represented by caring, professional lawyers, even Pro Bono.

Fighting an officer or officers on the road, you are already at a disadvantage because the officer can call for back up, you cannot. He or she would end up transporting you to jail while your car is towed. Another unreasonable expense. Make tomorrow better than the past.

Be special. Go to the nearest police station and say hello. Call Papa Johns and pay for a free pizza delivery to the station to show you care. Invite one officer in your district to a family re-union, Go, and ask if you can bring your child, children to the station to learn about policing. You might be surprised what you'll find. **You have more than fifty percent chance of winning in the courts**, and one hundred percent chance that you will lose on roadside's righteous litigation. Remember, you win only when you don't litigate your rights on the roadway. Peace!

www.ingramcontent.com/pod-product-compliance
Lightning Source LLC
LaVergne TN
LVHW040521210926
848480LV00007BA/1548